Amazon FBA

SIMPLIFIED

How to save time and money Selling Private Label!

Bimpe Sama

Subscribe at Substack:

https://www.substack.com/@Anxious ForNothing

Watch on YouTube:

https://www.youtube.com/@Anxious ForNothing

ANXIOUS FOR NOTHING.

Amazon FBA SIMPLIFIED

ISBN 9798863134154

CONTENTS

Introduction

Are you interested in learning how to sell on Amazon but need help figuring out where to start? Do you want to know how much it costs to make £10k monthly? Have you considered investing in that expensive course advertised on YouTube?

Look no further. This book is your perfect guide as a UK-based beginner. You'll learn how to run a successful private label business on Amazon (Fulfilled by Amazon) FBA. Then, afterwards, you can decide if you want to spend hundreds on videos and a supportless Facebook group.

Whether you're just beginning your journey or already have some experience, this book offers something new. For beginners, it serves as a comprehensive starting point, providing step-by-step instructions, guidance, and the opportunity to document your learning. So, all your notes will be in one place.

If you're already familiar with the basics, consider this book a valuable revision tool with workbook options to help you organise your information and product research in one place.

I understand that experienced sellers might find some of the information obvious. However, while this book caters specifically to beginners, there is an added section on AI that even seasoned sellers may find helpful.

Now, let's delve into ways we can sell on Amazon.

Amazon is a popular eCommerce platform that allows customers to purchase products in various categories, including food, books, clothing, toys, and home furniture.

As a seller on Amazon, you gain access to a customer base ready to spend their money. The conversion rate for Amazon Prime products stands at an impressive 74%, compared to a mere 3.32% for the top 500 merchants (source: DigitalCommerce360.com). Customers trust the Amazon brand; you can leverage that trust to maximise your profits as a seller.

The FBA business model makes it all possible; with FBA, Amazon takes care of picking, packaging, and delivering your products once they are purchased. With numerous warehouses nationwide, Prime members can receive their orders on the same day. Moreover, Amazon handles customer returns, saving you time and effort.

Imagine selling unlimited units per day without the hassle of packaging and shipping. Of course, there is some interaction with customers, mainly through responding to their queries, and Amazon provides a 24-hour window for replies.

While FBA is an excellent option for many sellers, there are cases where products are too heavy or don't meet FBA requirements. This is where the Fulfilled by Merchant (FBM) business model comes into play. In the FBM model, you, as the seller, are responsible for shipping items directly to the customers.

This model works well if you already have a warehouse

or have access to a third-party logistics provider. However, it involves the time-consuming task of wrapping and sending items from your home. I resorted to FBM due to high storage costs during the 2020 pandemic because a significant portion of my products remained unsold after several months in the warehouse.

It's important to note that this book covers the FBA business model, which offers a more efficient and cost-effective solution.

Now that you know the different business models, let's explore the three main ways to sell on Amazon using the FBA model.

Retail/ Online Arbitrage: This involves going to large stores to find products to sell at a profit. However, this approach can be time-consuming and costly due to the need to visit multiple stores.

Online arbitrage, on the other hand, allows you to search for products from the comfort of your device, making it a more convenient option.

Wholesale: The second method is wholesale, which requires ordering products in large quantities from registered wholesalers. Although cheaper to start than private label, wholesale can present challenges, such as multiple sellers competing with listings of the same product.

Private Label: Finally, we have the Private Label model, which is the most expensive and rewarding. With Private Label, you source a lucrative product from a manufacturer and place your own brand on it. This model gives you complete control over the listing, allowing you to protect your brand and optimise visibility by using relevant keywords.

Now, let's discuss why I wrote this book.

After attending countless free webinars, I realised they did not contain enough information to help me make an informed decision. I was repeatedly bombarded with sales pitches urging me to buy courses worth thousands of dollars for a limited-time discounted price. I purchased up to three courses, hoping the next one would be better.

It was frustrating, and I wanted to create a resource to empower aspiring Amazon sellers with all the necessary knowledge upfront. That's why I wrote this book—to ensure you clearly understand what you're getting into before making any commitments.

What sets this book apart is its practicality. You can use it as a learning tool to help you determine if Amazon FBA is the right path for you. At the end of sections one and two, you'll find questions and exercises that act as a guide, helping you conduct research and navigate launching your first Private Label product.

Additionally, at the end of the book, you get a breakdown of the total operating cost and cost of goods for your first year based on one product. As you progress, you'll get a rough idea of the investment required to launch your products in your first year. I'll give the total figure in the resource section, and you can see how much I spent in my first year.

When I described my Amazon journey to friends and

family, they urged me to write it so they could use it to start theirs. Once they started, they always appreciated my honesty and openness about the process.

To further support your journey, I've included links and details of resources I've used. These are suggestions to give you a starting point, but I encourage you to conduct your own research before making any decisions. Remember that the Amazon seller landscape constantly evolves; better options may emerge after reading this book.

After you've completed the book, I encourage you to refer to the notes you've written. Use them to hold yourself accountable and stay motivated. Remember, by the end of this book, I promise to equip you with the knowledge needed to make an informed decision about selling on Amazon.

So, if you're ready to embark on this exciting journey and discover the world of Amazon FBA, dive into the pages of this book. Let's start by unlocking your potential as an Amazon seller.

SECTION ONE: What Most Beginners Overlook

CHAPTER 1 Maximise Your Potential

Picture this: I was once a learner driver, brimming with excitement and a thirst for knowledge. I believed driving was simply about moving a car from point A to point B. Little did I know that this misconception would lead me to fail my driving test. Everything fell into place when I realised that driving entailed seeing the road through a completely different lens. A fundamental shift in mindset was the key to effortlessly passing the test.

Mindset shift

Starting a new business follows a similar pattern. It demands a fresh way of thinking that sets us apart from the crowd. Think about it - when we delve into the world of Amazon FBA, we embrace the role of an entrepreneur and become masters of our own destiny. We're used to being employees, having undergone years of traditional schooling that shaped our thinking and told us when to start working. Hard work became our mantra, and giving up was never an option.

However, the challenge lies in viewing the same road differently. As entrepreneurs, we face challenges head-on, taking calculated risks rather than avoiding them. The most crucial mindset shift involves redefining our perception of failure - it must become a stepping stone toward success.

As you embark on this new journey, I want to challenge you to seek ways to change your mindset. Start by immersing yourself in books and videos that explore the entrepreneurial mindset. Entrepreneurs think differently from those with an employee mindset. They view problems as opportunities, as each obstacle presents a chance to find a solution we can monetise. In contrast, an employee mindset focuses on avoiding trouble and potential income loss.

New Habits

I'm not here to claim that one mindset is superior. Instead, as business owners, we need a different approach to challenges if we want to thrive. In his book Atomic Habits, James Clear explains the power of making small daily changes to our habits. I read his words, implemented his advice, and was astounded by the results. With a busy lifestyle and family responsibilities, I had to carve out protected time to dedicate to my new business. Remember, success won't materialise overnight - it requires consistency.

Our Reason Why

Finding motivation is essential at the start of any journey. We all begin with enthusiasm and boundless energy when we embark on something new. So, let's establish why you want to sell on Amazon. What truly motivates you? It could be financial independence, escaping the 9-to-5 grind, spending more time with family, or the freedom to explore the world. Take a moment to answer this question and discover your personal motivation.

If your immediate answer is to make more money, let's dig deeper using a powerful technique called The Five Whys, developed by Sakichi Toyoda, a Japanese inventor and founder of Toyota Industries. By repeatedly asking "Why?" we can uncover the root of your motivation. For example:

Why do I want to sell online? "To make some extra money".

Why do I want to make some extra money? "To have more financial security".

Why do I want more financial security? "To reduce my dependence on a single source of income".

Why do I want to reduce my dependence on a single source of income? To have more control over my financial future and be less vulnerable to economic uncertainties.

Why do I want more control over my financial future and be less vulnerable to economic uncertainties? To feel empowered and free to pursue my passions and dreams without financial constraints.

By using The Five Whys technique, we can uncover a more profound desire for financial security, independence, empowerment, and the pursuit of a fulfilling life. Understanding this root motivation will help you prioritise your actions, stay focused, and devise effective strategies. It will also serve as a source of encouragement on challenging days or when you need an extra energy boost.

The approach is everything. How we perceive and think about a situation directly impacts the outcome. Before diving into the world of selling on Amazon, it's crucial to understand the mindset required. Challenges, frustrations, and unexpected costs will inevitably arise. How we approach these situations will determine the outcome. In the next chapter, we'll explore the common reasons for failure. By developing the right mindset, you'll be better equipped to navigate the challenges and achieve success on your Amazon selling journey.

CHAPTER 2 Set Up For Success

"It's too late to join Amazon," they say. "It's saturated." I've heard this sentiment multiple times, and it's not uncommon for beginners to feel discouraged by the sheer number of sellers on Amazon. In 2019, there were over 281,000 sellers on Amazon FBA in the UK, according to Statista.com. And that number continues to grow. But let me ask you this: How many of those sellers genuinely understand what they are doing? How many of them are making a profit of over £5,000 per month in their first year? The reality is that many of them fail, often due to avoidable mistakes.

But here's the good news: You don't have to be one of them. By understanding the common reasons businesses fail, you can avoid the pitfalls and set yourself up for success. This chapter will explore five common pitfalls beginners encounter when selling on Amazon FBA. More importantly, I'll provide actionable solutions to help you overcome these challenges and believe in your ability to succeed.

Lack of Business Acumen

Many beginners start selling on Amazon without fully understanding what it means to own a business. Unlike being an employee, where you have set tasks and someone to hold you accountable, owning a business requires a different mindset. It involves upfront investment, delayed gratification, and reinvesting profits for greater rewards.

Solution: **1.** Take time to complete the worksheets in this book. **2.** Invest your time in understanding best practices for running a business. **3.** Expand your knowledge by reading books on financial freedom. Doing this will help you develop the business acumen necessary for success.

One Thing to Implement: Complete the worksheets in this book and commit to investing time in learning about business principles.

Underestimating the Level of Effort

I've seen success on Amazon portrayed as straightforward. "Follow three simple steps: one finding a lucrative product, two sourcing it from Alibaba, and three selling it on Amazon FBA". It sounds simple, but it requires substantial effort.

Beginners often fail to differentiate their products and create copycat products without any improvements, which leads to fierce competition and lower profit margins.

Solution: Your product must solve a problem and offer improvements over existing options. Dive into section two, the product research section of this book, to learn how to find the right product and differentiate it effectively.

One Thing to Implement: Ensure your product solves a problem and offers improvements over existing options.

Quality Control

Many newbies fall into the trap of finding a manufacturer on Alibaba and shipping products without conducting thorough testing and quality control. This oversight can result in purchasing poor-quality products and facing delays and challenges during shipping and customs clearance.

Solution: Request samples and carry out inspections for every large shipment. Explore section three, the product sources, suppliers, and shipping, to learn how quality control.

One Thing to Implement: Request samples and hire an inspection company for every large shipment to maintain product quality.

Effective Product Listing and Promotion

Simply getting your product into Amazon's inventory is not enough. You need customers to find and buy your product. With a well-optimised listing and effective promotion strategies, your product may stay active in the warehouse, accruing storage fees.

Solution: Run a product launch campaign and optimise your product listing with relevant keywords and professional images. Learn more about product listing and detail creation in section four of this book.

One Thing to Implement: Run a product launch campaign and optimise your listing with keywords and professional images.

Financial Management

Making money is one thing, but managing and keeping it requires financial literacy. Unfortunately, traditional education often neglects to teach financial skills, leaving many individuals ill-equipped to handle finances effectively.

Solution: Understand your profit margin and the operating costs of running your business. Dive into Chapter 7 for creating the profit plan and shipping and Chapter 3 for starting up your business to gain knowledge on financial management.

One Thing to Implement: Understand your profit margin and your business's operating costs.

The Power of Guidance

As a bonus, I've included guidance. The internet provides free information about Amazon FBA Private Label, and AI tools like ChatGPT can help. However, sifting through conflicting information and validating the credibility of the information can take time and effort.

Without proper guidance, you may stumble into pitfalls, such as having a great product but a poor listing or losing money due to hijackers.

Solution: This book serves as a valuable resource to start your journey, providing processes, templates, and hard-to-find information without the hefty price tag. However, it's still essential to seek guidance from an experienced mentor who can review your listing, keep you accountable, and provide advice tailored to your journey.

One Thing to Implement: Use this book as your foundation and find an experienced mentor to guide you.

Now that we understand the mindset required to run a successful Amazon business, it's time to delve into the next chapter. We'll explore the various business models available and help you choose the right one. This knowledge will give you an advantage over most beginners who overlook the legal and tax implications of running a business.

CHAPTER 3 Choose Your Model

Welcome to Chapter 3 of this Amazon selling guide, where we'll discuss the importance of choosing the right operating model for your business. This decision will shape the legal and financial aspects of your Amazon business. I understand the challenges and considerations you must make at this stage. So, let's dive in and help you make an informed choice that aligns with your goals and aspirations.

Operating models

Sole Trader: Quick Setup, Personal Liability

If you're looking for a quick and straightforward setup process with minimal paperwork, operating as a sole trader might be the right option. As a sole trader, you'll be personally responsible for the business's income, which will be taxed at your individual tax rate.

However, one crucial aspect is that your personal assets are liable to legal issues or business debts.

Limited Company: Legal Formalities, Asset Protection

On the other hand, setting up a limited company involves more legal formalities and administrative tasks. You'll need to appoint a director and register the company name, ensuring compliance with tax and financial regulations. The advantage of a limited company is that your business becomes a separate legal entity, protecting your personal assets. This means that your assets won't be at risk in the case of legal disputes or business debts.

My Experience and Recommendations

When I started my Amazon journey, I began as a sole trader operating from home. At that time, I didn't want my address displayed on Company House (in the UK), a requirement for limited companies. However, I later discovered that from as little as £13, I could register my own limited company and use services that provide an alternative address for Company House. This motivated me to switch to a limited company structure. Still, it was an administrative nightmare before Amazon changed my account information.

Deciding Your Amazon Account Type

As a seller on Amazon, there are two main types of accounts to consider. First, we have the individual seller account, which charges a modest fee of around £1 per item sold. On the other hand, we have the professional seller account, which comes with a monthly fee of approximately £30. While the professional account carries a higher cost, it also offers additional privileges - making it the ideal choice for private-label merchants, which we'll focus on here.

To minimise initial expenses, I opted for the individual seller account. This decision was driven by the fact that it took me over three months to find and order my product. I didn't want to commit to the monthly fee until I had the goods in my hands. Once I received my sample test batch and felt confident proceeding, I switched to the professional account. This allowed me to create my listing and begin selling my batch. Looking back, a more strategic approach would have been to order the sample test batch first and then open my Amazon Seller account.

Once your Amazon account is running, you can expand your reach and sell in other countries. It's worth investigating any tax implications associated with selling abroad. If you venture into international markets, you must link your Amazon account to a company like Payoneer. This payment service provider helps facilitate transactions by receiving foreign currency and converting it into your local currency, enabling easy transfers to your bank account.

Take a moment to consider the name you want to give to your Amazon store. This may seem like a small detail, but it holds significant importance regarding branding - something we'll delve into later. It's worth noting that Amazon rewards sellers with registered brands by granting them additional privileges. So, don't underestimate the impact of choosing a solid and memorable name for your store.

As we progress through this book, we'll delve deeper into the power of branding and how it can set your business apart. But for now, let's move forward confidently, armed with the knowledge of the different Amazon account types and their implications for your journey as a seller.

Opening Your Amazon Account

If you're new to selling on Amazon, establishing your business before opening an Amazon seller account is the first step. This involves legally setting up your business and obtaining a tax reference number. In the UK, you'll need a Unique Taxpayer Reference (UTR) number, while in the United States, it's an Employer Identification Number (EIN). I vividly remember how long it took me to acquire these numbers, so I understand the challenges you may face. Don't worry; we'll navigate through it together.

In addition to the tax reference number, there are other information you'll need to provide when setting up your Amazon seller account:

Personal Details: Your name, email address, phone number, and a unique password for your account. These details will help Amazon identify you as the account owner.

Business Details: Provide your legal name, address, and contact information. This information is essential for customer correspondence and order fulfilment.

Business Model: Determine whether you'll operate as a Sole Trader or a Limited Company. This choice will impact your legal and financial responsibilities, so it's essential to understand the distinction.

Bank Account: You'll need a dedicated bank account to receive payments from Amazon. Consider opening an online-only account, as they often have lower fees than traditional brick-and-mortar banks. Moreover, you can easily link it to free accounting software, simplifying your tax-related activities.

Credit Card: Have a valid credit card to pay Amazon seller fees. This ensures a smooth transaction process and lets you start selling without hiccups.

It's worth noting that Amazon now conducts an online interview as part of its verification process. Stay updated on their website to be aware of any new requirements or changes in the process.

Remember, opening your Amazon seller account is the gateway to opportunities. Take the time to gather all the necessary information, and don't hesitate to seek help. Together, we'll lay the foundation for your successful journey as an Amazon seller.

Managing Your Finances and Accounting Basics

If you're anything like me, the business finance and accounting world can feel like learning a whole new language! To make things easier, I've created a handy worksheet that you can use at the end of this section. Don't worry if you're already familiar with the basics; I didn't fully grasp their significance when I started my own business. Despite making good money, I struggled to keep hold of it, and that's why I urge you to continuously grow and improve your financial literacy.

Let's dive into accounting basics - the not-so-thrilling side of the business if you ask me! While you could hire an accountant or bookkeeper, reducing costs is crucial during these early stages. So, adopting good practices that save you time and effort when tax season rolls around is best. Trust me, in the future, you will be grateful for this foresight.

Some business bank accounts offer free accounting software integration. Take the time to research, find the best option for you, and make the most of this opportunity. Personally, I use an online-based business bank account that doesn't charge me transaction fees. In return, I get free accounting software integrated if I make just one monthly transaction.

Alternatively, you can opt for a manual approach. Spreadsheets or free solutions like QuickFile can help you stay organised. Regardless of the method you choose, it's crucial to maintain records of your expenses, statements, and sales.

Regarding expenses, keep every receipt, including charges for your account. Some examples include:

- Amazon fees
- Launch costs
- Cost of goods sold
- Software tools fees
- Training and FBA courses

Scanning and keeping electronic copies of these receipts for easy access is best.

Keep a dedicated folder for all your bank, credit card, and Amazon statements. Additionally, do the same for all your products on Amazon and other platforms.

During my first year in business, I handled my bookkeeping. However, as I grew, I hired an accountant for tax filing and Company House submissions. Once I started using accounting software, my bookkeeping process became seamless. Every quarter, I would download my statements and sales data, inputting them into a spreadsheet to avoid the last-minute hassle at year-end. This proved particularly helpful because, after six months, my bank would often only provide PDF copies of statements.

Mastering your business finances and keeping accurate records is essential for long-term success. Adopting good accounting practices from the start will save you countless headaches and ensure a solid financial foundation for your business. Let's conquer the numbers together!

Branding: Creating a Connection with Your Customers

Branding is more than just a label on your product; it's how you want your business to be perceived by customers. As we embark on our Amazon selling journey, it's essential to start with the end in mind and consider our brand alongside product research. Building a brand allows us to establish associations and connections with our customers, setting us apart from the competition. Let's dive into the steps for creating a brand and explore the privileges that Amazon offers to brand-registered sellers.

When conducting product research, thinking beyond your initial product is essential. Imagine you're selling chopping boards in the Kitchenware category. Alongside the chopping board, consider what other products could complement your brand. These additional products should align with your main product and contribute to building a cohesive brand. Once customers are satisfied with the chopping board, they'll naturally turn to you for related products. As your brand gains recognition and value, you can gradually increase your prices.

Now that you have your products in mind, it's time to think about a suitable brand name and a name for your Amazon seller account. Some sellers opt to keep their brand name and seller account name the same, which is perfectly fine. However, if you decide to explore different niches in the future, you may want a separate seller account. Alternatively, you can choose a non-descriptive name for your seller account, like Nike,

Virgin, or Amazon (pun intended!). Let's look at popular types of brand names for inspiration:

Descriptive names: Like hotels.com, clearly communicate what your brand is about, like hotels.com. However, they can be challenging to trademark.

Evocative names: These names require a brand story or association to help customers connect, such as Dove. They are easier to trademark.

Invented names: Create your own word, like Google, which has become synonymous with searching. These names are enjoyable to explore and have no trademark competition.

Lexical names: Often a play on words, like Whiskas, sometimes related to the product or niche. They can involve intentional misspellings or combining words, like AirBnB.

You can also consider acronyms, geographical references, or even using the founder's name as part of your brand.

Once you have a brand name, checking if it's trademarked is crucial. You can use the search database on WIPO.int; I've included the link in the resources section of this book. Additionally, secure your domain name and social media handles using namecheck.com to ensure consistency across platforms. You also need to brainstorm taglines and themes that align with your brand's identity and then work on your logo. Platforms like Fiverr.com offer affordable options for logo creation.

Amazon Brand Registry is a valuable program that offers numerous benefits for brand-registered sellers. While the cost of getting trademarked registered worldwide can be around £3k, it's a worthwhile investment. Once you have a trademark, Amazon provides exclusive privileges to boost sales and protect your brand. Here are some advantages of Amazon Brand Registry:

A+ Content: Enhance your product descriptions with engaging text and images.

Sponsored Brands: Advertise three products at the top of the search results page, displaying your logo.

Store Pages: Create a dedicated page to showcase your range of products and promote your brand.

Project Zero: Ensure the removal of counterfeit listings, safeguarding your brand's reputation.

Early Access: Gain early access to new features and rollouts, staying ahead of the competition.

By leveraging the power of branding and taking advantage of the Amazon Brand Registry, you can establish a strong presence on Amazon and create a meaningful connection with your customers.

Wrapping Up and Looking Ahead

This chapter discusses the importance of choosing a suitable operating model and account type for your Amazon business. We've also touched on the significance of branding and the benefits of the Amazon Brand Registry. Branding needs to be thought of in tandem with your search. Chapter 4 will focus on product selection.

Remember to keep the momentum going and embrace the learning process. Your dedication and effort will pave the way for success on Amazon.

Section One Worksheet

Mind Shift Exercise

Becoming a business owner means you are the boss and no longer an employee. We must view the same road differently, like moving from students to qualified drivers.

Consider how you'll tackle the following as an entrepreneur. Then, complete the sentence in the space below.

When I come across a challenge,

I will….

Once I've calculated and mitigated against possible risks

I will…

When something doesn't go as planned

I will…

New Habits Exercise

James Clear, author of Atomic Habits, explains that small changes yield significant results. For example, spending 20 minutes every day learning an instrument could mean you have mastered the basics by the end of the month.

What three changes can you make to create time to work on your business?

1

2

3

Name two things you will keep doing to help your business.

1

2

Is there one thing you can do to support your business?

1

The Five Whys Exercise

The Five Whys is a technique to understand the root of our motivation. Motivation keeps us going and focused in moments when things become challenging.

Answer the following question: Why am I selling my Private Label brand on Amazon?

1st Why Answer...

....

....

Then, ask yourself why four more times and write the final answer below.

5th Why Answer...

....

....

Operating Model Exercise

There are two main operating models for running a business. As part of becoming a business owner, you'll need to decide if you would like to operate as a sole trader or a limited company.

Research the difference between a sole trader and a limited company. Create a list of the pros and cons for each based on:

- Level of paperwork
- Legal liabilities
- Tax considerations
- Any other area you found helpful in your search (optional).

Based on your needs, decide on which option is best for you. Use the list of the pros and cons of each choice to help you decide.

I will Operate as…

Finance Fun

Let's have some fun as we learn accounting terms. The answers are in the resource section.

Created using the Crossword Maker on TheTeachersCorner.net

Across

2. Total value of owned items and investments.

5. The return on an investment, often expressed as a percentag

7. Day-to-day expenses incurred to keep a business running.

8. Identification number used in the UK for customs purposes

10. Money received from customers.

Down

1. Profits after all expenses are deducted.

3. The total profit before deducting expenses.

4. The amount of money a business receives in cash.

6. The flow of money into and out of a business.

9. Amount owed to a business.

Section Two: Obtaining the Perfect Product

CHAPTER 4 What You Need to Pick a Winner

How did you find the worksheets? You're already making progress by completing section one, which is fantastic! Now, as we move on to section two. I want to share something important with you while searching for the perfect product. It's not worth your time and effort to search for a product that promises £500-£1k in profit per month and then try to manage 10 of these products to reach your £10k monthly target, which is how I tried to start out.

Handling ten products singlehandedly can be challenging. Instead, let's focus our energy and time on finding products that generate £5k-10k in monthly profit. Once you've found one of these winners, add two more products in the same niche to your catalogue. Doing this will increase your authority among your existing customer base, which you've already established with your first item.

You'll need to use specialised search software tools like AMZScout and JungleScout to discover these high-profit products. This will be your first significant investment in your business. While manual product research is an option, it can be time-consuming, and your competitors who use software will always have an advantage over you. These tools are faster, allow you to search multiple categories, and provide up-to-date criteria to stay ahead of the game.

Product categories

Good news! When it comes to selling on Amazon, there are several categories where you can start selling right away. I focused on the baby category and specialised within a specific area to provide a targeted solution. However, it's important to note that there are certain products that you cannot sell through Amazon's FBA program. As of this publication, these include hazardous items such as firearms, ammunition, and fireworks, which are flammable, explosive, or corrosive in nature.

Additionally, some products have restrictions and require approval from Amazon before you can sell them. Examples of regulated items include alcohol, tobacco, and prescription drugs. It's worth mentioning that Amazon FBA does not support the sale of perishable goods or oversized items.

Some categories require approval from Amazon; you need to fill in an approval form, which may be accepted or rejected. These categories include beauty products and cosmetics, jewellery, and clothing.

This book will focus on the categories where you can sell on Amazon FBA without restriction or approval application. Currently, these categories include:

- Art and craft
- Baby products (excluding clothing)
- Kitchen and home
- Lighting
- Garden and outdoors
- Industry and Scientific
- Office products
- Lawn and garden
- Pet supplies
- Home Improvement
- Toys and games
- Sporting goods

Remember that Amazon FBA is constantly evolving, so reviewing their guidelines is essential before starting your product research. Additionally, it's advisable to check if your product has any restrictions on selling outside your country of operation.

Research criteria

Finding a winning product is like having a secret recipe for success. It's the key to providing a long-lasting solution for your customers. Here are the guiding principles to consider when searching for that winning product:

Weight: Look for products that weigh less than 1.9kg to minimise shipping costs.

Dimensions: Opt for products with dimensions of approximately 45x34x26 cm to reduce storage fees.

Sturdiness: Choose sturdy products that are less prone to breakage to minimise damage during transit and returns.

High Demand: Focus on products with a low Best Seller Ranking (BSR), indicating increased demand.

Year-Round Appeal: Select products that sell consistently throughout the year. Avoid seasonal items connected to events like Diwali, Easter, or back-to-school.

Competition: Aim for niches with at least three private label sellers, ensuring a healthy level of competition.

Research Software and Tools

While you could manually browse the best sellers list for your chosen category, using a product search and analysis tool saves time and provides valuable insights. These research tools generate a list of products that meet your criteria in your chosen niche. They offer information such as:

Low Competition: Products with fewer than 300 reviews indicate low competition.

Keyword Volume: Products with a keyword volume of 10k monthly searches indicate demand.

Sales Volume: Products with competition making more than 10-15 sales per day.

Profit Margin: Products with a profit margin of at least 30% after considering Amazon fees and cost of sales, allowing you to assess the investment potential.

Revenue Comparison: Products where the competition makes at least twice your desired monthly revenue.

Examples of product research software include AMZScout*, JungleScout, SellerApp, and Helium 10. Some of these tools offer free trials, which you can take advantage of. Then, after this, you can invest from £300 for an annual subscription or pay roughly £41 which lasts for a month, and, like Netflix, cancel and re-subscribe.

Another approach to product research involves utilising Amazon Keyword research or PPC (Pay-Per-Click) advertising. This helps you understand customer search behaviour and identify niches with fewer sellers, which can be advantageous for market entry.

Furthermore, AI-powered tools like ChatGPT can help you find profitable products, and we'll explore these options in detail later in the book. Most product search software also provides a ready-made product bank for your convenience.

I used AMZScout, which offers a Chrome extension. It analysed my personal purchases in the background and displayed a number in the bottom left-hand corner, indicating if the niches met most of my set criteria. I'll include links in the resource section for easy reference.

Differentiation

Now, dedicating time to this section is genuinely worthwhile. It will make you stand out, especially from those who find profitable products from Alibaba and ship them to Amazon. This area can be challenging for individuals working alone. While you can find information online, having a mentor to guide you with your specific product is invaluable.

Differentiation is your secret weapon for gaining a competitive edge. Your product needs to offer a solution and provide value to the customer. To achieve this, we'll explore various methods to differentiate your products and make them truly stand out.

Customer Complaints: Consider customer complaints as liquid gold. As discussed in the mindset section, problems present opportunities for finding solutions. Look at the product reviews and identify recurring themes across different sellers. Is there a chance for improvement? Can you suggest changes to the manufacturer, such as altering the size, shape, or design to address the problem? Shulex is an AI software that can analyse reviews and provide feedback on potential product improvements.

Bundling Options: Sometimes, solving a problem might involve considerable spending. Bundling different modifications and testing them can be a great approach. You can explore opportunities to sell two or more items in the same niche together as a set. Have you ever noticed the "Customers also bought" section when purchasing from Amazon? This suggests potential things you can bundle together. However, remember that others may copy the idea, so being the first to do it gives you an advantage.

New Variation: Consider introducing a different shape, size, or colour of the same product. For example, improved handling or a larger size. Emphasise the value and highlight these enhancements in your product listing.

New Markets: Research how the product is performing in other countries. Are there higher demands in markets where few sellers have entered? This could be an opportunity to enter and dominate the market before others catch on. If it's a non-English speaking country, ensure accurate translation and account for cultural differences.

Branding: Branding is another area where you can differentiate yourself from the competition. Main competitors might neglect branding, especially if they enter an emerging niche. Sometimes, the brand name and product don't align. Seize this opportunity to showcase that your product is more reliable.

Consider improving the packaging - can you do a better job or get a design that attracts customers? Take a page from Apple's book, as they excel at packaging their products.

You don't need to go for expensive packaging products, but you can make them unique enough to be part of your product's selling point.

Improved Listing: Evaluate your product listing. Does it align with your branding? What improvements can you make? Do the descriptions and images effectively sell the product? Are there any conflicts between the listing and customer complaints? For instance, if the product claims to be durable, but the customers complain that it lasted a few months.

We now know the winning criteria for finding a product and the various selling categories. Let's dive into Chapter 5, where we'll explore how the AI tool ChatGPT can assist us in our journey.

CHAPTER 5 Boost Your Productivity 10x with AI Prompts

Are you concerned about Amazon's saturation and intense competition? Do you worry that it's too late to start and you missed the opportunity? Well, let me assure you that things are constantly improving, and there will always be good opportunities to enter the Amazon marketplace. And now, with the power of artificial intelligence (AI), you can even surpass those who have been in the game for years.

When I started my business, I had to write and double-check my listings. But now, we have AI, such as ChatGPT, to assist us. Our job is to review and personalise the AI-generated content to align with our brand. The exciting part is that you can also use an AI called MidJourney to create captivating social lifestyle images for your products. Gone are the days when I had to hire models and photographers, as this can now be done in two minutes.

Limitations of AI

It's important to understand that ChatGPT AI has its limitations, and there are a few things to keep in mind:

Limited Data: The free AI model is trained on data collected until 2021, so it may have a few recent information.

Hallucination: Occasionally, the AI may generate inaccurate or irrelevant responses. It's essential to exercise caution and verify the information.

Quality of Prompts: The quality of the responses depends on the quality of your prompts. The more knowledgeable you are and the better you can articulate your prompts, the more accurate and valuable the AI-generated responses will be.

You gain a significant advantage by combining AI with your Amazon product search tool. Many established sellers may not have embraced AI yet, allowing you to stay ahead. Additionally, you'll be far ahead of new sellers still following outdated YouTube videos.

Now, let's look at the top 20 Amazon prompts that are typed into ChatGPT:

1. How do I start selling on Amazon?

2. What are the best practices for optimizing Amazon product listings?

3. How can I increase my Amazon sales?

4. What are some effective strategies for Amazon PPC advertising?

5. How do I handle negative customer reviews on Amazon?

6. What is the Amazon Buy Box, and how can I win it?

7. How do I calculate Amazon FBA fees?

8. What are the requirements for Amazon Brand Registry?

9. How can I improve my Amazon SEO?

10. What are the benefits of using Amazon Sponsored Products?

11. How do I create a successful Amazon storefront?

12. What are some effective ways to launch a new product on Amazon?

13. How can I deal with counterfeit or unauthorised sellers on Amazon?

14. How do I handle Amazon suspensions or account issues?

15. What are the best tools for Amazon sellers?

16. How can I protect my intellectual property on Amazon?

17. What are the steps to conduct product research for Amazon FBA?

18. How do I optimise my Amazon product images for better conversions?

19. What are the requirements for Amazon's Buy Box eligibility?

20. How can I differentiate my private label products on Amazon?

These prompts cover various topics and can help you with your Amazon selling journey. However, it's worth noting that using AI prompts for differentiation will truly set you apart. By crafting unique and specific prompts, you can uncover innovative ideas and solutions that your competitors may have overlooked.

Ready-made Prompts

Below are examples to get the best out of the tool and a prompt model. Replace the text in bold with your own information.

Create Listing Prompt: You are a six-figure Amazon Seller. Can you provide me with 5 bullet points describing the features and benefits of **[product name]**? Include the following keywords **[list keywords]**. Write in a style that a 9-year-old can understand.

Find Keywords Prompt: You are an Amazon customer. Can you provide me with a list of 10 keywords used over 1000 per month to search for **[product name]**?

Product research Prompt: Can you list 5 Keywords that Amazon customers use over 1000 times weekly to find a product? The product makes over **[desired amount]** in monthly sales and has at least three sellers.

Seller Central Complaint Prompt: You are an Amazon seller contacting Seller Central. Can you write a concise and polite message asking for support with my **[missing products/ specific issue]**?

Customer response Prompt: You are an Amazon seller replying to this complaint **[paste complaint].** Write a concise response of 200 words to the customer. It must be polite and considerate.

Niche identification Prompt: List a product searched for over 1000 times per month by **[customer type or description]** that they don't always find.

More ways to leverage ChatGPT include creating social media and advertising content and analysing reviews to identify valuable opportunities.

Prompts play a vital role in setting you apart from the competition. Over time, you can refine and improve your prompts to achieve better results. If you don't get the desired response initially, you can always perfect and iterate your prompts to get the desired outcome.

Let me illustrate the power of a well-crafted prompt. It's what I used to improve my introduction for this book.

> *Prompt:* I've written an introduction to an Amazon book that helps beginners understand what is required to sell on Amazon, the effort, time, and mindset based on my selling experience. Review my introduction and improve it based on 1 the problem I solve. 2 the solution I give. 3 show my credibility. 4 the benefits the reader gains. 5 give the reader proof. 6 bring out the promise I make. 7 prompt them to read. Keep my tone friendly and use simple and easy-to-read language that flows:[paste intro]

The result was light years better than my original. You

can compare the two. I've included the original introduction I pasted into ChatGPT in the reference section.

It's important to note that the free version of ChatGPT doesn't use live data. For product research, always combine it with your product research tools to access accurate and up-to-date information.

Another useful AI tool worth exploring is Midjourny, an image AI generator that operates through Discord. By uploading an image of your product along with a detailed prompt specifying what you want, such as lighting or a photo-realistic look, you can utilise Midjourny's capabilities. The more description you provide, the better the results. Start your prompt in Discord with "/Image," followed by a detailed description and a link to your product image. For example, let's say you are selling a portable barbeque grill and require an image of people using the grill and having fun on a picnic. Once you add the link to your uploaded image, add the prompt describing the scenery and setting where your product would appear.

The AI landscape is rapidly evolving, with numerous new tools being introduced. For instance, Opus Clip is a tool that can transform long content into engaging video shorts. Shulex, as mentioned earlier, is a powerful tool for analysing Amazon reviews. While ChatGPT remains a primary tool, others like Midjourny, Opus Clip, and Shulex offer unique capabilities. To stay updated on the latest AI tools, you can visit websites like FutureToolsAI.com and Futurepedia.io, which provide directories of AI tools.

However, it's crucial to remember that AI tools like ChatGPT are just one piece of the puzzle. The following section will delve into the critical topic of sourcing products from the right manufacturers and navigating the shipping process. This step is essential for ensuring the success of your Amazon business. So, let's proceed and discover how to find the perfect manufacturers and efficiently ship your products!

Section Two Worksheet

Product Ideas Exercise

Here is a checklist to get you started on product research. Some product research tools allow you to save products you found on your profile, or you can keep a spreadsheet or list.

Action	Due	Done (tick)
Set My monthly profit goal £....		
Purchase Product research software		
Find 20 -15 unrestricted products that meet the research criteria		
Select 10 - 5 with strong opportunities for differentiation or improvements.		
Write down the opportunities for differentiation or improvements.		
Select 5 - 3 that can solve the main customer complaints.		
Find 10 keywords on 3 - 2 products		
Decide your first and second product.		

Amazon FBA SIMPLIFIED

Section Three: Sourcing & Shipping

CHAPTER 6 How to Pick a Credible Supplier from Alibaba and Not Get Ripped Off

Great! Now let's dive into finding the perfect manufacturer for your product and ensuring their credibility.

Finding a Supplier

Regarding finding manufacturers, Alibaba.com is the go-to website for most people. While many manufacturers are familiar with Amazon sellers, keep in mind that they might be in a different time zone. It's essential to communicate with them politely and using simple language.

You can also explore trade shows or search for local manufacturers, but for this book, we will focus on Alibaba.com, a platform I have experience with.

To start your search, you can use the product search software I mentioned earlier, which provides links to manufacturers of your desired product. Alternatively, you can visit Alibaba.com and apply the following criteria to filter your search for the right manufacturers:

- Trade Assurance

- Verified supplier/Onsite checked

- Gold supplier/4.5 rating

- Minimum of 2 years on Alibaba

- Possess relevant product certifications

- Possess relevant management certifications

Make sure to only reach out to suppliers that meet these criteria. Then, utilise the website filters to narrow your selection to around 20 potential suppliers. Contact and further evaluate 5 to 3 suppliers that you find most promising.

When conducting your search, remember to add the term "OEM" at the end of your search query. For example, if you are looking for flashlights, search for "Flashlight OEM." It stands for Original Equipment Manufacturers. This will filter out resellers and display factories that manufacture your desired items.

Contacting the Supplier/Manufacturer: When initiating contact, use polite and simple language while being specific about your requirements. The goal is to establish a good relationship with the manufacturer from the start. Manufacturers want to feel confident in your capabilities, so avoid giving the impression that you are a solo seller. They must trust that you will bring them recurring business and have the necessary funds.

When I started, I projected the image of being part of a larger organisation because manufacturers tend to believe that companies have more financial resources. This approach will give you leverage during negotiations, as you can refer to your boss wanting to reduce costs. If they perceive you as a lone seller, they may try to maximise their profits at your expense.

To showcase your knowledge and experience, here are some quick-fire questions for you to answer:

What does EWX mean?

Clue: This will help you separate shipping costs effectively.

What does DDP mean?

Clue: It ensures your goods arrive at the right location with covered costs.

What does OEM mean?

Clue: Manufacturers providing this service can build products based on your design, packing, branding logo, and instructions.

What does ODM mean?

Clue: Manufacturers offering ODM services create products that you can private label.

What does MOQ mean?

Clue: Understanding MOQ will help you plan your costs and determine the number of units you can order.

When contacting the supplier for the first time to request a quote, feel free to use the following template on the next page. Remember to maintain a polite and simple tone:

Subject: Inquiry for **[Product Name]**

Dear [Supplier/Manufacturer's Name],

I hope this message finds you well. My name is **[Your Name]**, and I represent **[Your Company Name]**. I came across your company profile on Alibaba.com and was impressed by your range of products, mainly your **[specific product]**.

I am interested in sourcing **[specific quantity]** of **[product name]** with the following specifications: **[specifications/details]**. Please provide a detailed quotation, including the unit price, shipping costs, and other applicable charges. Additionally, I would like to know your minimum order quantity and estimated production time.

Please note that I am looking for a long-term partnership, and if everything goes smoothly, we have the potential for recurring orders in larger quantities. Therefore, I value excellent communication, high-quality products, and competitive pricing.

Thank you for your attention to this matter. I look forward to your prompt response. If you require any further information, please do not hesitate to ask.

Best regards,

[Your Name] [Your Company Name]
[Contact Information]

Remember, it's crucial to personalise this template. Use polite and simple language throughout your communication.

Samples

Now, let's dive into the crucial step of getting samples from your potential suppliers and testing them to determine the viability of your product.

Before placing a large order, order samples from your potential manufacturers. This allows you to test the quality of their products and assess how well they sell. Some sellers even order samples from multiple manufacturers before deciding on their final supplier.

You have a few options when it comes to samples. You can order a sample and thoroughly examine it yourself without listing it on Amazon. If you are satisfied with the quality, you can skip running a sample test batch and immediately proceed with a large order.

I opted for a sample test batch, and here are the steps I took:

After exchanging a few messages and building rapport with the supplier, let them know your boss wants to order samples for quality checks and inspection.

Inquire about the price for express delivery to show seriousness and urgency. Remember that depending on the weight, the cost of express delivery may exceed the cost of the product itself!

Request a sample batch of around 50 units (or a number that suits your budget and the product's weight). Ordering a larger batch will give you a better idea of the product's consistency. Assure the supplier that you will place a much larger order once your boss approves the sample.

Have the sample batch shipped to your address so that you can thoroughly examine the products.

Please take pictures of the samples to create your Amazon listing and label them appropriately for shipment to Amazon.

If the manufacturer is unwilling to send a sample batch, check if the product is available on AliExpress. Remember that the sample test batch will not have your logo and may need branded or simple packaging. In this case, you should place the products in individual jiffy bags or boxes before shipping them to Amazon.

Once Amazon receives your product, it's recommended to set a lower price than the competition initially. As your product begins to sell, gradually increase the price. If you reach a point where sales decline, consider reducing the price. The two-week test period aims to determine the optimal selling price range.

Note the highest and lowest prices you could sell your product. Additionally, running a pay-per-click (PPC) campaign is vital during this test period. This campaign will give you insights into how your product is selling without any promotions or reviews.

In my experience, I started with a budget of £10 per day for automatic PPC and adjusted it based on performance. I reviewed which keywords performed best and manually increased the funding. Some days, I reduced the budget to £5 based on what I could afford. I strongly recommend having a mentor, receiving PPC training, or seeking assistance from platforms like Fiverr.com, as PPC can be a highly effective but potentially costly area, especially for beginners.

The two-week test period will provide you with valuable data and insights. Use this information to decide whether to proceed with a larger order. You'll also gain insights into potential improvements for your listing or product. If you're making sales in the first few days (I was selling 2 - 5 units per day in my first week), you can initiate the process for a large order. If not, your listing may hinder your sales, and you can adjust or tweak your PPC strategy accordingly.

The goal of the test period is to gather data, and making a profit or breaking even during this time is a bonus. Selling the sample batch will give you an idea of your daily sales potential and optimal price range. It also provides practice for shipping products to Amazon and creating listings, which can boost your confidence in the process. Additionally, this test phase allows you to determine if you've successfully filled a gap in the market and resolved key customer issues.

Following these steps will give you confidence and valuable insights to guide your decision-making process as you move forward in your Amazon selling journey. The next step is to ship your products to Amazon.

CHAPTER 7 From Order Fulfilment to Amazon Warehouse

Once you've finalised your order and are ready to ship your products from China to Amazon, there are a few important steps to follow. Let's dive in!

If you ordered a sample test batch, you must label the products at home before sending them to Amazon. However, it's best to ask the manufacturer to handle the labelling for a large batch, a product launch, or restocking. Another option for large orders is to send them to an Amazon FBA prep centre. The prep centre will check and label each product before forwarding it to Amazon. Once you've created a listing on Amazon, you can obtain the necessary labels.

Creating Your Profit Plan

You'll need specific details from your manufacturer to create a profit plan. These include the production lead times, production costs, shipping costs, and management fees on Alibaba. In the resource section of this book, I will provide a link to the spreadsheet I used. Here are the details you'll need:

- Number of units

- Total cost to produce (EXW)

- Total cost to ship to Amazon

- Alibaba fees

- Custom Tax

- Inspection fees

- Any other production costs

- Packaging costs or Amazon prep centre fees

Add up the above presales costs and divide the total by the units you ordered. This will give you the cost per unit for production and shipping to Amazon. This figure is crucial in determining your profit margin. Next, gather details on Amazon fees per unit and PPC (pay-per-click) budget per unit.

Add your cost per unit to the Amazon fee and PPC budget per unit. This final figure represents how much it will cost to sell each unit. This figure should be two-thirds of the unit price to make it worthwhile. For example, let's say it costs £5 per unit to get the product to Amazon, and the combined Amazon fee and PPC budget is £7. The average of £5 and £7 is £6. So, to make a profit of at least £6, you'll want to sell your product for at least £18. We will discuss PPC in more detail later, but it's worth noting that £3 is considered expensive for a keyword. You want to be confident that customers will make a purchase. Otherwise, it's best to find a more cost-effective keyword.

Inspections: Before shipping your products, it's essential to conduct an independent inspection to ensure their quality. I prefer to do this on-site in China to address any issues directly with the manufacturers. I use an inspection company based in China (details are in the resource section). They checked the product's labelling, quality, and packaging. It was a live inspection, and I felt like I was in the manufacturer's warehouse in China, although miles away in the UK. Finally, they ensured it was safely on the ship!

Alternatively, you can ship your products to an Amazon prep centre, where they will remove any faulty items. Both approaches help reduce the chances of returns and negative reviews. It's worth accounting for inspection costs in your profit plan.

Shipment Options: Shipping by sea is generally the most cost-effective option, but it does take more time. You can arrange for a freight forwarder to collect your products from the factory. With this method, you pay EXW (Ex Works) to the manufacturer. This is the method I used for my large order and product launch.

If the freight forwarder cannot collect from the manufacturer's location, you can consider FOB (Free on Board). In this case, the manufacturer ensures that your products are loaded onto the freight forwarder's boat. Obtain quotes from at least three companies, and check if your manufacturer can offer a competitive price.

Another option is DDP (Delivered Duty Paid), which I used for my sample test batch and reorder. With DDP, your goods arrive at your desired location with all the duty fees paid. This allows you to send the products directly to an Amazon prep centre or the Amazon warehouse.

Other modes of shipping include Air, which is the most expensive and the fastest. This option is suitable for receiving sample batches or a small quantity while the main order arrives by sea.

Shipment Planning on Amazon Seller Central

Once you've determined your best shipping option, it's time to fill out your Amazon shipment plan. You can find this option under "Manage Inventory" in Seller Central. Locate your listing and click on "Send/Replenish Inventory." Select "Create new shipping plan." This informs Amazon to prepare for receiving your goods. Below, I've listed the details you'll need and with a description.

Location of goods: The address the goods are coming from. This could be from the Manufacturer, Amazon prep centre or your home.

How goods are packed: Select **1.**"Case-packed goods" if you sent a single product with no variations. **2.** If you have variations, select "Individual products." **3.** If you didn't label your units, choose "Amazon to label."

Unit amount: Enter the number of units you are sending. You can give your shipment a name if you prefer.

Delivery Info: Complete the delivery method. I used a freight forwarder for my first large batch and selected "Pallet." In most cases, small parcel delivery should suffice.

Amazon has partnered with UPS, so I recommend using them if you can obtain a reasonable price and if they can collect from your manufacturer prep centre or home. If you choose UPS, Amazon will provide you with a code to use on the UPS website, and Amazon will charge the fee to your seller account. There is no need to pay UPS separately. Select "Collection" on the UPS site and paste in your tracking numbers, separated by commas if you have more than one box.

Consignment details: For shipment packaging, provide the number of boxes you are sending, the number of items in each package, their weight, and dimensions. Once you've reviewed and approved the shipment plan, you can print the labels and send them to whoever will be shipping your products to Amazon (your manufacturer or the Amazon prep centre).

Below is a 10-step summary for shipping our product by sea to the UK. This is the most cost-effective option for your large batch.

Step 1: Obtain an EORI (Economic Operator Registration and Identification) Number from https://www.gov.uk/eori/apply-for-eori before you start. This is essential for customs clearance.

Step 2: Prepare Shipping Labels. Log in to your Amazon Seller Central account. Go to 'Inventory' and select 'Manage FBA Shipments.' Create a new shipment plan for your products.

Step 3: Complete Shipment Details. Enter the shipment details, such as shipment name, ship-from address, and number of cartons. Make sure to follow Amazon's guidelines and provide accurate information. Your manufacturer will be able to give you details on the number of units in each carton, the total number of boxes, and the dimensions and weight.

Step 4: Label Your Shipment. Download and send your labels to your manufacturer. Once your product has been made, they will affix the labels to each product with a unique SKU (Stock Keeping Unit) or FNSKU (Fulfilment Network Stock Keeping Unit). This ensures accurate tracking and handling of your products.

Step 5: Get Freight Forwarder Quotes. Visit websites like Freightos, Flexport, or Shipa Freight to get quotes from freight forwarders. Provide details of shipment source and destination - the Amazon warehouse they will deliver to. They'll help you plan the shipping process and provide cost estimates.

Step 6: Inspect your product. Book an inspection once you have a date from the manufacturer when your products will be ready for shipment. Ensure faulty items are replaced or the cost is reduced.

Step 7: Prepare Shipment Contents. The inspection company will ensure your products are securely packed in cartons and well-protected. You can request any required packaging materials to prevent damage during transit.

Step 8: Know About Customs and Duty Fees. Understand that customs and duty fees may apply when importing goods. You can get this information from the UK government's official customs website or consult a customs expert.

Step 9: Book Shipping with a Freight Forwarder. Once your shipment is labelled and ready, contact your freight forwarder to book the sea freight. Please provide them with the necessary details and documents, such as the EORI number and shipping labels.

Step 10: Monitor Shipment Progress. Keep track of your shipment's progress using the tracking information provided by the freight forwarder. Once your shipment reaches the UK, you must handle customs clearance. Once it reaches the Amazon warehouse, Amazon will take care of the rest.

Remember, the process might seem overwhelming at first, but taking it step by step will make it manageable. If you have any questions or concerns, contact Amazon Seller Support. Good luck with your sea shipment to the UK!

Now that you've completed the shipping process, you're one step closer to launching your product on Amazon. In the next section, we'll discuss the exciting journey of launching your product and getting it in front of potential customers. Stay tuned, and keep up the great work!

Section 4: Launching Your Product

CHAPTER 8 Product Listings & Detail Creation

Congratulations on reaching Chapter 8! This chapter will explore the exciting journey of producing your product and understanding the importance of keywords in optimising your Amazon listing. Let's dive in!

Once your samples arrive, it's time to capture their essence through photography and create your Amazon listing. While some sellers may copy and paste images from the Alibaba website, I encourage you to take a different approach. Differentiate yourself and add your brand's personal touch. Your Amazon listing is like your space at the supermarket counter, surrounded by other related products and competition. Your goal is to stand out and attract buyers. The keywords, images, title, additional images, bullets, and description must convince them to choose your product.

The Power of Keywords

Now, let's understand the importance of keywords. As an Amazon seller, keywords are the words that best describe your product, including its solution, colour, size, material, and even the type of customer or event associated with it. For example, "birthday gifts for him/her." These keywords are crucial in helping customers find the products they are looking for.

Think about the last product you purchased on Amazon. How did you find it? You likely typed words associated with the product into the Amazon search bar. The search results then displayed products that matched your search terms.

Let's consider an example. Imagine a customer needs a replacement battery for a food scale. They know what the battery looks like and what it's for, but they might not know its specific name. In this case, they would enter keywords like "flat circle batteries" or "food scale batteries" into the search bar. The actual product they need is a lithium coin battery. But unless you know its name, you wouldn't type that in the search bar.

It's crucial to ensure that your listing includes these relevant keywords so that Amazon knows how to display your product to potential customers. Without using high search volume keywords, your product may have limited visibility and not appear on the first page of search results. High search volume keywords are those used to search for products over 1000 times per month. We must strategically incorporate these keywords into our titles, bullets, descriptions, videos, images, and backend. However, we need to be cautious not to spam by using excessive or irrelevant keywords. The keywords should flow naturally within your title, bullets, and description while still capturing the essence of your product.

By effectively utilising keywords, you can significantly enhance the visibility and discoverability of your product on Amazon, ultimately attracting more potential customers.

Product Photos

When selling on Amazon, your product photos are crucial attracting customers and securing conversions. Let's explore the different types of product photos and their significance.

Main Photo: Your main photo is customers' first impression of your product on the search results page. The image determines whether they will read your title, scroll past, or click to learn more. Amazon has specific guidelines for the main photo: it should be on a white background, with the product occupying 85% of the frame. Avoid including text, logos, or badges, except for what is on the packaging, which is better showcased in other listing photos.

The main photo must be a high-resolution image taken in good lighting. Transparency is vital, so ensure that it accurately represents what the customer will receive. Aim for a resolution of 1000 x 1000 pixels for optimal quality.

Lifestyle Image: A lifestyle image captures your product being used in its natural environment. For example, if you're selling a portable BBQ stove, show it being used on camping trips, at the beach, or in a home garden. Showcase people enjoying the product, creating a connection with potential buyers.

Infographic Image: An infographic image conveys how your product solves a problem or provides a solution. It should cover the key points customers need to know, reducing the need to read through the bullets and description. Use text, graphics, and badges that align with your brand's design. Highlight the main selling points, such as ease of setup or features that make it easy to clean and store.

Specifications Image: Since customers are buying online, they may need help gauging the size of the product. Show the product from different angles if necessary and provide measurements to give a clear idea of its dimensions.

"How to Use" Image: Include an image demonstrating the process if your product requires assembly or unfolding. Consider incorporating a video to provide a visual guide. Another option is to show a before and after, highlighting how your product solves a problem or improves a situation.

Differentiation Image: Some sellers use comparison charts to showcase why their product is the best solution. If you have modified your product to set it apart from the competition, illustrate these differences in your photos.

Product Title

The product title is the next crucial element after your main image. It's what potential buyers read before selecting your product, and its goal is to entice them to click through to your product detail page. Here are some guidelines to follow when crafting your product title:

Length: You have a maximum of 200 characters for your title. Keep it concise and impactful.

Capitalisation: The first letter of every word should be capitalised, except for words like "for," "in," and "and."

Information to include: Your title should contain the following elements while maintaining a natural flow:

Name of Brand: Include your brand name to establish brand recognition and credibility.

Keywords: Incorporate relevant keywords that best describe your product and its features.

Name of product/purpose: Clearly state the name or purpose of the product to provide clarity to the buyer.

Features of product: Highlight key features that make your product unique and desirable.

Value: Convey the value proposition or benefit your product offers the customer.

Solution/Benefits: Emphasize the solution your product provides or its benefits to potential buyers.

Example of use: Provide an example of how the product can help customers visualise its application.

Variation/Specification: Include this information in the title if your product has different variations or specifications.

Who it's for (if applicable): If your product caters to a specific target audience, mention it in the title.

Amount (if applicable): If relevant, include the quantity or size of the product.

For example, let's consider the product title for a portable BBQ:

> Title: EasiGrill Foldable Portable Tabletop Gas and Charcoal BBQ Grill | Durable Stainless Steel for Outdoor Cooking Camping or Garden Patios | 18inch Silver.

In this example, "EasiGrill" represents the brand name, attracting buyers seeking a hassle-free solution. Keywords like "Grill" and "Portable BBQ" are included. "Foldable," "Portable," and "Tabletop" address the buyer's needs for a compact and easy-to-carry grill that can be placed on a table. "Gas and Charcoal" highlights the product's features. "Durable Stainless Steel" communicates the value of the product. "Outdoor Cooking Camping or Garden Patios" specifies the use scenarios. Lastly, "18inch Silver" indicates the size and colour variation.

By incorporating these elements into your product title, you can create a compelling and informative title that captures the attention of potential buyers.

Video

Videos are a powerful tool for providing customers additional insight into your product. They offer a visual representation that helps customers understand your product's dimensions and solution. It's important to note that this feature is available to brand-registered sellers, so if you're not, check if Amazon has made this feature available to you.

When creating a video, it's best to focus on one aspect of your product. You can choose to create a lifestyle video, a demonstration video, or even a comparison video. Keep the video between 30-45 seconds and include royalty-free music. Avoid directing customers off Amazon to third-party sites or including promotional information such as discounts or offers. By testing different types of videos, you can determine which format generates the most sales, whether demos or lifestyle-focused videos.

Bullets

Your bullet points play a crucial role in highlighting your product's main benefits and features. They should be short, descriptive, and include organic keywords.

With up to five bullets available, prioritize the benefits and features that are most important to your customer. If your product fills a gap in the market, this is the perfect opportunity to mention it. I recommend leading each bullet with a feature in capital letters, followed by a colon to make it stand out. Utilise the remaining characters to explain in detail the benefits, how your product solves a problem and the enhancements you've made. Your goal is to evoke emotion and appeal to values, such as being reusable or made from recycled plastic. Your bullets should compel the customer to make a purchase.

Descriptions

Product descriptions are your last push to convert the customer into a buyer. Incorporate keywords throughout the listing and address your customer's concerns and main complaints. Emphasize product features and their benefits, and include a strong call to action. If you're brand registered, you'll have access to templates that allow you to include images and text, known as A+ Content descriptions.

Backend

While customers won't see the backend of your listing, there are crucial elements that will have an impact on your listing's success. One is a Universal Product Code (UPC) barcode obtained from the GS1 website. This barcode is necessary for physical products and is also used for selling in brick-and-mortar stores. It's important to note that Amazon requires a UPC as part of your product listing. Additionally, you'll need to set up your Fulfilment Network Stock Keeping Unit (FNSKU), which helps Amazon identify your product and link it to you as the seller. Ensure you attach your FNSKU to each unit before sending them to Amazon FBA. Your SKU (Stock Keeping Unit) number will also help you manage your inventory significantly when scaling and offering multiple variations of the same product. It's worth mentioning the Amazon Standard Identification Number (ASIN), which identifies the product itself.

In conclusion, you can use AI to build your listing, saving you from scratching your head or hiring someone on platforms like Fiverr.com (which I've done before!). Look for product search tools that offer this option and consider leveraging ChatGPT. Most product search tools provide high search volume keywords, which you can utilize when creating your listing. However, I still believe it's valuable to take the time to understand what makes a good listing. This knowledge will help you ask the AI the right questions and verify its output.

CHAPTER 9 Product Launch and Ranking

For beginners, getting your product to page one of the Amazon search results and making sales can take time and effort. In this chapter, we will cover key points on how to rank your product, use promotional tools, and improve your chances of success. By following these steps, you will connect with your audience, inspire belief in your abilities, and show them that results are possible. Let's dive in and discover how to take your Amazon business to the next level.

To get listing visibility, it needs to be robust and optimised. This means including all relevant keywords and using high-quality images. In addition, running a Pay-Per-Click (PPC) campaign can significantly boost your visibility. We discussed PPC in detail under product sourcing and suppliers. If you conducted a sample test batch, you already have some data on the best keywords for your product. However, you can follow the same process if you order a large batch directly.

When I started, I ran a PPC campaign targeting specific keywords. I priced my product lower than the competition to attract my first few sales. It's essential to tweak your listing to find what increases sales continuously. Look at your competitors. Does your title include the most popular keyword? Are people clicking through but not buying? Can you improve your images or bullet points?

If you want to delve deeper into PPC, you can explore resources like Fiverr.com or watch YouTube videos on how to master it. Remember, PPC requires daily attention and adjustments. Without proper guidance and training, you can lose money without tangible results. However, once you master Amazon's Search Engine Optimization (SEO), you'll be on the right track.

When selecting keywords to target, I chose those with a bid range between 50p and £2.50. Ensuring these keywords are relevant to your niche and product is crucial. Keep a close eye on them and monitor your spending regularly. Set a daily cap to avoid overspending and maintain control over your budget.

PPC Basics

Here's a quick guide on how Amazon Sponsored Ads works to get you started. I've based the figures on a product selling 15 units per day. Adjust the guide to suit your budget.

Step 1: Finding Relevant Keywords

Start by understanding what keywords potential customers might use to search for products similar to yours. You can find relevant keywords in several ways:

Amazon's Search Bar: As you start typing in the search bar, Amazon suggests popular search terms. These are often great keywords to consider.

Product Listings of Competitors: Analyse the listings of successful competitors to identify the keywords they are using.

Keyword Research Tools: Tools like Amazon's Keyword Planner, Helium 10, or Jungle Scout can help you discover high-potential keywords.

Step 2: Using Long and Short-Tailed Keywords

Short-Tail Keywords: These are short and general phrases (1-2 words) that capture a broader audience. Example: "running shoes." Use these when you want to cast a wider net, but be prepared for higher competition.

Long-Tail Keywords: These are longer, specific phrases (3+ words) that target a more niche audience. Example: "Women's lightweight running shoes for marathons." Use these when you want to reach people with a specific intent, often leading to higher conversion rates.

Negative Keywords: These are short or long-tail keywords you don't want your product to appear for. For example, "Men's shoes" or "Men's running shoes" if you wanted to target women.

Step 3: Set Daily Budgeting

For products selling 15 units daily, consider allocating a daily budget of around 20-30% of your product's sale price. So, if your product sells for £20, you might start with a max daily ad budget of £6.

Step 4: Capitalising on High-Performing Keywords

To make the most sales from your keywords:

Monitor Performance: Regularly review your ad performance metrics. Amazon provides data on:

- Impressions – the number of customers your ad was shown to.
- Clicks – the numbers that then decided to click

on the ad
- Click-through rate (CTR) – Clicks divided by Impressions. You want above 0.5%.
- Cost per click – you'll want to keep this low.
- Ad Cost of Sales (ACoS) – you'll want it below 30%.
- Conversion rate – the percentage that went on to purchase after clicking on the ad.

You can run two types of PPC campaigns: automatic and manual. As of writing this book, 10-15% is a reasonable conversion rate on Amazon for PPC.

Keyword Optimisation: If you identify keywords with a high CTR but low conversion. You should adjust your product listing to match customer expectations better. Otherwise, remove the ones costing you money and not making sales.

Negative Keywords: Exclude irrelevant search terms as negative keywords to avoid wasting the budget on irrelevant clicks.

Bid Adjustments: Increase bids on keywords generating sales. See if you can get them at a lower cost. Reduce bids on ones that don't make as much sales. Pause keywords that are not delivering sales.

A/B Testing: Experiment with different ad copy and images to see what resonates best with your audience.

Seasonal and Trending Keywords: Capitalise on seasonal or trending keywords to boost sales during specific periods.

Remember, success with Amazon Sponsored Ads takes time and experimentation. Continuously optimise your campaigns based on data and adjust your strategy as you learn what works best for your products and target audience.

Promotions

Bringing external traffic to Amazon can give you a significant boost in rankings. As of 2023, social media and AI have become powerful tools for promoting your Amazon products. Consider various ways to generate traffic outside Amazon's platform.

For example, you can utilise Google AdWords alongside Amazon PPC. Identify your target audience's preferred social media platforms, like Pinterest, Instagram, or TikTok. You don't have to tackle all these platforms simultaneously. I created a Facebook page to target my audience. Choose the platforms you can manage effectively and focus on them. Unlike when I started in 2019, we now have the advantage of using AI to create content and speed up the process.

Another effective strategy is collaborating with influencers. Ask them to create YouTube shorts you can leverage on Amazon Inspire. Inspire is an in-app shopping feed that uses short-form videos to encourage Amazon customers to explore their shopping interests and discover new products. This is available for you if you are brand-registered. Otherwise, you can approach an influencer.

Combining AI and social media will give you an edge in 2023 and beyond.

Within Amazon, you have access to promotional tools. You can create coupons and discounts to incentivise customers to buy your product. Initially, I started with discounts, and once I found my optimum selling price, I offered coupons.

You can also explore selling your product on discount sites like Jumpsend, owned by JungleScout. They also provide a customer mailing system to help you obtain reviews. Here's a list of other services that offer similar opportunities:

- My Seller Pal
- Viral Launch
- AMZ Tracker
- Zonpages

Amazon also offers a service called Vine Reviews Amazon, which serves the same purpose. Another action you can take to encourage reviews is to include a thank-you note inside your packaging. Express appreciation to your customers and kindly prompt them to leave a review or reach out with any questions. However, refrain from asking the customer to leave a positive review specifically. This is against Amazon's Terms of Service, and your account may be suspended or permanently banned if the customer reports you.

This may seem obvious, but I'll spell it out – never offer incentives to your customers for leaving a positive review. This is a bad business practice, first and foremost, and against Amazon's T&C. Sourcing reviews should not put your entire business in jeopardy.

Product Reordering

As part of inventory management, tracking how long it takes to manufacture and ship your product to Amazon is essential. Additionally, keep a record of your average sales per week. Let's say you sell an average of 60 units per week over three months. When you reach the 750-unit mark, it's time to start reordering.

When placing your orders, it's beneficial to inquire about other products your manufacturer may sell. Especially when making a reorder, they might have a new product coming out. It's also worth finding out what their best sellers are. This information will help you stay competitive and ahead of the market. Don't forget to negotiate for a price reduction at least once.

Lastly, pay attention to Chinese national holiday periods when placing your orders. These holidays can have an impact on shipping times. For instance, National Day in October could affect Q4 Christmas sales.

By understanding the strategies and techniques covered in this chapter, you will be better equipped to launch your product successfully on Amazon. Remember, it's a journey of learning and improvement.

The next chapter will delve into scaling your business, so stay tuned and keep up the great work!

CHAPTER 10 Scaling Your Business

Congratulations on successfully launching your first product and reordering it. It's time to scale your business by expanding your product line. This chapter will cover the steps you need to take to grow your Amazon business and achieve long-term success. Remember, repetition is vital to building a thriving enterprise. Let's dive into strategies to help you scale your business effectively.

Thorough Research and Untapped Opportunities: Maintaining success requires thorough research to identify untapped opportunities and confirm demand for your following products. This step ensures that you choose products with the potential for profitability and growth. Take the time to understand market trends and consumer preferences in your niche.

Establish Strong Relationships and Optimise Inventory Management: Maintaining strong relationships with reliable manufacturers and suppliers ensures smooth production and shipping. Effective inventory management is crucial. Stay organised and track the time it takes for your product to be manufactured and shipped to Amazon. By optimising this process, you can minimise delays and keep your listings active.

Build a Strong Brand Presence: Invest in building a strong brand presence. Focus on creating high-quality product listings, professional product photography, and engaging content. Staying within one product category and building a brand around it is recommended. This consistency will help you establish credibility and gain customer loyalty.

Increase Product Visibility: To scale your business, you must increase your product visibility on social media and through Amazon PPC campaigns. Drive targeted traffic to your listings by utilising platforms where your target audience hangs out. Keep refining your PPC strategies to maximise your return on investment and generate more sales.

Track and Analyse Key Metrics: Track and analyse key metrics such as conversion rates and customer reviews. These metrics provide valuable insights into your product's performance and customer satisfaction. Use the data to make data-driven decisions and continually optimise your listings for better results.

Expand Your Product Line and Enter New Markets: Expand your product line as you grow and consider selling on Amazon's other markets, including the US, EU, and Asia. This diversification can create new opportunities for sales and revenue streams. However, make sure to thoroughly research and understand the regulations and requirements of each market.

Ensure Inventory Availability: Running out of stock can negatively impact your listing and rankings. Use the inventory management tool in Seller Central to stay on top of your stock levels. Be aware of any potential supply issues and have backup plans in place. If you anticipate delays, consider gradually increasing your prices over a period of time, but be cautious to avoid upsetting the Amazon algorithm. Having your own private label allows you to set prices that align with your brand's value.

Customer Satisfaction and Staying Informed: Keep customer satisfaction at the heart of your business. Respond to inquiries promptly and proactively address any issues that arise. Amazon constantly evolves, so stay updated with the latest trends and policies. Attend Amazon webinars and network with other sellers to stay informed about industry changes and seize potential opportunities, such as receiving investment offers for your brand.

Amazon Seller Central

To conclude this chapter, let's briefly cover Seller Central. The web interface where you manage your Amazon business. Here are some essential functions you can perform:

Product Listing: Create and manage product listings, including descriptions, images, pricing, and inventory levels.

Manage Orders: View and process incoming orders,

including payment processing, printing shipping labels, order fulfilment, returns, and customer service inquiries.

Manage Inventory: Monitor and track inventory levels set up automated replenishment, and receive alerts for low stock to ensure you never run out of inventory.

Performance Metrics: Access reports on sales data, customer feedback, and seller feedback to identify areas for improvement and optimise your performance. You can also download reports for regular accounting purposes, such as monthly statements and Amazon fees.

Advertising and Promotions: Create and manage advertising campaigns, such as Sponsored Products and Sponsored Brands, to increase product visibility and drive traffic to your listings. Utilise tools to set budgets, select targeting options and analyse advertising performance.

Customer Communication: Use the Buyer-Seller Messaging system to communicate with customers, answer inquiries, resolve issues, and provide post-purchase support. Remember to respond within 24 hours to maintain a good seller reputation.

Performance Notifications: Stay updated with important notifications regarding policy changes or issues affecting your account or listings. Take necessary actions based on these updates. For example, Brexit significantly impacted me, and staying informed helped me navigate the changes.

Additionally, you can integrate various software into your Seller Central account, such as accounting, listing creation, and foreign currency payout. If you encounter any issues with your listings or account, Seller Central is the go-to platform to seek support.

By following these strategies and utilising the functions of Seller Central, you'll be well on your way to scaling your Amazon business and achieving long-term success. Keep rising and repeating the steps for continued growth and profitability.

Conclusion

Congratulations on reaching the end of this book! I hope you've found the information you were seeking and are feeling empowered to take the next step on your Amazon FBA journey.

Launching your Amazon business is a journey that requires the right mindset. Your willingness to put in the work and your belief that you can do it go a long way in helping you weather the tough times. This book highlighted the importance of the right mindset and the steps necessary to make your Amazon journey a reality.

It is not always enough to know what to do – you also need to know what NOT to do. Common pitfalls that new sellers fall for can seem small, but they can be costly. Don't let your Amazon business fail before you really start. Finding your footing means avoiding the pits and stumbling blocks that have held back other sellers. Be cautious even as you undertake this new venture.

And if I have to highlight the most crucial point, it's this – keep a close eye on your finances. I have provided an approximate cost of launching your product, but you must also be diligent. Hidden costs can run high if you are not careful, especially costs associated with research tools, setting up the business, and mentorship. Plan out and monitor your investment, no matter how small the price may seem. If you haven't yet, check out the resource section to see how much I spent in my first year.

Throughout this book, I've maintained a practical approach. It serves as a learning tool, giving you a comprehensive understanding of Amazon FBA and allowing you to determine if it's the right path for you. I've experienced the frustration of attending webinars that lacked valuable information and being bombarded with sales pitches for costly courses.

Before we part ways, I recommend finding a mentor to guide you on your journey, especially for your first product. Joining a community of successful Amazon sellers is also essential, as this journey can be lonely. If you choose to take a course, ensure it offers more than videos. Look for mentors who have achieved success, check if their students are successful, read reviews about them, and see if they provide one-on-one sessions and update their materials. Consider their experience, longevity, and whether they still sell on Amazon. Lastly, make sure you resonate well with them.

I've shared my own Amazon journey with honesty and

openness. Many friends and family members encouraged me to write it down so they could use it to start their own businesses. I'm grateful for their support, and I hope that by sharing my experiences, I've been able to provide you with valuable insights into the process.

In addition to the practical advice, I've included links and details of resources that I found helpful. These serve as a starting point for your research, as the Amazon selling landscape is constantly evolving, and new options may emerge when you read this book.

As you move forward, I encourage you to refer to the notes you've taken while reading. Use them to hold yourself accountable and stay motivated on your journey as an Amazon seller. Remember, this book promises to equip you with the knowledge needed to make an informed decision about selling on Amazon.

Now it's time to unlock your potential as an Amazon seller. I believe in your ability to succeed. Take action, embrace the challenges, and stay persistent. Remember that selling on Amazon requires effort, time, and a positive mindset. Results are possible if you approach this journey with determination and a willingness to learn.

Thank you for joining me on this exciting adventure. I wish you all the best as you embark on your Amazon FBA private label journey. Believe in yourself and let your entrepreneurial spirit shine. You've got this!

About Me

Let me share a bit about my Amazon journey. I started with retail and online arbitrage, using it as a stepping stone to build confidence and learn the ropes of shipping to Amazon warehouses. However, with three boys and a full-time job, I had no time to visit shops.

In December 2018, I experienced success when my sample test batch sold out within two weeks. This motivated me to place an immediate order of 300 units, which arrived in April 2019 by sea. I invested in a logo, hired a photographer, and got a model for my lifestyle images. I adjusted my listing and expanded my sales to Europe.

I became brand registered after spending £3k, which in hindsight, could have been used for a second product. Unfortunately, after the successful launch, I faced a setback. My product sold out, but I didn't have enough cash flow to reorder on time. One of my biggest mistakes was a lack of focus. I spent another £3k on various courses, but only a couple were related to selling on Amazon.

I made money from the 300 units and then misspent much of it! As a former employee-minded entrepreneur, I highly recommend taking time on wealth management. I read about this in the Psychology of Money. This is another excellent book I recommend you read.

When I finally managed to reorder, I encountered several setbacks that led to over six months of delay. First, the manufacturer got the colour wrong, and then there were delays due to a Chinese national holiday in October and shipping issues.

Once my goods reached Amazon in early 2020, I faced the challenges of Brexit and the Covid-19 pandemic. Being a high-end product targeted towards parents with children under two years old, a significant portion of my sales were in the EU. Amazon changed its shipping policies from the UK to the EU, resulting in additional paperwork and confusion. We were all learning together, as everyone was affected. Looking back, I should have reinvested my profits into a second product, diversifying my business.

Below is a breakdown of what I spent in my first year:

INCOME STATEMENT
FOR THE PERIOD FROM 20 DECEMBER 2018 TO 31 DECEMBER 2019

	2019 £
Turnover	10,965
Cost of sales	(7,094)
Gross profit	3,871
Administrative expenses	(6,946)
Operating loss	(3,075)
Loss on ordinary activities before taxation	(3,075)
Tax on loss on ordinary activities	-
Loss for the period	(3,075)

After selling all my products, I decided to take a break. Like everyone else, the impact of 2020-2021 was significant.

I've started a YouTube Channel and mailing list alongside writing this book. The goal is to keep me accountable and add value. I work in IT as an Agile Delivery Manager. I love my faith, planning, efficiency, budgeting and achieving goals!

My goal this year was to get this book out and start a YouTube Channel! On the channel, I focus on planning and setting goals. What is your goal? I would love to get you started. My YouTube is https://www.youtube.com/@AnxiousForNothing.

Many thanks, Bimpe.

Resources

Thank you for your time. Please leave a book review on Amazon to help others.

https://Amazon.com/review/create-review?&asin=B0CKPL84GP

Your Google Sheets product profit plan is available for free in my welcome email when you subscribe to my newsletter at

https://anxiousfornothing.substack.com.

Breakdown of Costs

As the intro mentions, a breakdown of what you can expect to send in your first year on one product is on the next page.

The total comes up to about £8,752. This figure could be less based on how much you decide to spend on training. Also, you may choose to register your brand later. Remember, the customs charges will vary based on your product.

Item	One-off Cost	Yearly Cost
Setting up an LTD Company	£10	
Registered Office Service		£46.80
Product Research Software		£300
Amazon Course/ Mentoring	£1000	
UK Brand Registry	£480	
UPC barcodes	£60	
Amazon Professional Seller account		£360
Accountant filling service to HMRC and Company House		£250
Sample batch of 50 units including DDP shipping	£1000	
Professional product images	£35	
1000 units EXW at £4 per unit	£4,000	
Alibaba Trade Assurance Fee (3% of total order)	£120	
Inspection company I use	£150	
Sea Shipping of 1000 units to Amazon	£700	
Customs charges of 1000 units	£240	

Reference

Amazon conversion rates:

https://www.digitalcommerce360.com/2015/06/25/amazon-prime-members-convert-74-time/

James Clear, author of Atomic Habits

Morgan Housel, author of The Psychology of Money

Five whys:

https://kanbanize.com/lean-management/improvement/5-whys-analysis-tool

The number of Amazon sellers in UK:

https://www.statista.com/statistics/1086664/amazon-3p-seller-by-country/

Crossword Creator:

https://worksheets.theteacherscorner.net/make-your-own/crossword/

Useful Resources

Business name checker:

https://www.tide.co/company-name-check/

Setting up a company:

https://www.1stchoice-formations.co.uk/

Receiving foreign payments in local currency: www.payoneer.com

Check if trademarked worldwide:

https://www.wipo.int/reference/en/branddb/

Free accounting software:

 www.quickfile.co.uk

Freelance Websites (For PPC, packing and logo design)

- Upwork
- Fivver
- 99 Designs

Product research tools:

*My favourite tool is AMZscout because of its web extension. It provides me with ideas based on my personal purchases on Amazon. I contacted them to get discounts for you. I get a commission if you make a purchase at no extra cost to you.

• $15 OFF for monthly plan for the 1st
month:https://amzscout.idevaffiliate.com/i
devaffiliate.php?id=1933&url=3770

• 65% OFF your purchase of the AMZScout
bundle:https://amzscout.idevaffiliate.com/i
devaffiliate.php?id=1933&url=3771

• $20 OFF for annual
plan:https://amzscout.idevaffiliate.com/idev
affiliate.php?id=1933&url=3772

You are not obligated to make a purchase. Other good tools are:

- Jungle Scout
- SellerApp
- Helium 10

AI tools:

- **ChatGPT**
- MidJourney
- Opus Clip
- Shulex

Manufacturer websites:

- Alibabar.com
- AliExpress.com

Chinese-based Inspection Company:

https://fba.help/price

GS1barcode:

https://www.gs1uk.org/about-us/membership/get-a-barcode

Amazon professional account pricing:

https://sell.amazon.co.uk/pricing#selling-plans

Business name checker:

https://www.tide.co/company-name-check/

Trademark service:

https://trademarkwizards.co.uk/pricing/

https://www.voc.ai/how-to-analyze-amazon-reviews-using-ai

Freight forwarding costs:

https://www.freightos.com/

Alibaba fees:

https://activity.alibaba.com/ggs/trade_assurance.htm
l

Previous Introduction

This book is ideal if you want to find out what selling private labels on Amazon FBA entails, especially if you are thinking of paying hundreds for a course you saw advertised on YouTube. You'll have all the information in one place on where to start, where to go, and what to do.

If you have already started your journey, this book will act more like a revision book. Take advantage of the workbook options. So, you can hold all your information and product research in one place.

Are you an experienced seller? Then most of the information could be obvious. The aim of this book is for absolute beginners, but you may find the section on AI useful.

What is Amazon FBA

Amazon is an eCommerce website where customers can buy items from several categories, including food, books, clothing, toys, and home furniture. Amazon does this by providing a platform for sellers to sell their products to customers.

Customers come to Amazon ready to spend. The conversion rate for Amazon Prime products is 74%. This is impressive compared to 3.32% for the Top 500 merchants. This is according to DigitalCommerce360.com. This is because Amazon has built a brand that customers trust. As a result, sellers use this advantage to profit. Which you can also get a slice of!

Fulfilled By Amazon (FBA) is the business model making this possible. Amazon takes responsibility for picking, packaging, and delivering the seller's product once purchased. Amazon has many warehouses across the country. This means Amazon Prime customers can receive their item by the next, if not the same day.

Amazon also manages customer returns. This business model saves the seller time and effort as you can sell an unlimited amount of units per day. You are not wrapping and labelling items or waiting for the post person to pick them up. There is an element of interacting with the customers, this is often to respond to questions. Amazon gives you 24hrs to reply.

For some sellers, their product is too heavy or doesn't meet the requirements for FBA. This is the Fulfilled by Merchant business model (FBM). This means the seller sends out the item to the customer. This model works well if you already have a warehouse or are using a company that can do this for you. Otherwise, you'll have to wrap and send the items from home. I did this option for a while due to high storage costs. During the 2020 pandemic, my product sales dropped. A large amount has not sold after three months in the warehouse. This book will cover the FBA business model.

Amazon FBA Business Models

There are three main ways to sell on Amazon using the

FBA business model. More than one way to sell on Amazon FBA and make profits. Below is a brief explanation of them. This book covers the Private label model.

For all three models, you will send the items to the Amazon warehouse.

Retail/ Online Arbitrage

This is one of the least costly yet requires a lot of time. Retail arbitrage involves going into large supermarket stores and shops in person. The goal is to find products that you can sell at a profit. Often this means going into several stores to get large enough quantities. I found this time-consuming and costly to drive to several stores.

With online arbitrage, it's better. You can search for products from your device. The challenge comes when there are restrictions on the quantities you can buy. With both Retail and Online Arbitrage, you scan the product, then check if you can sell it on Amazon and if the profit margins make it worthwhile.

Wholesale

Wholesale is cheaper to start compared to private label. Unlike arbitrage, you can order large quantities. Like private label, you'll search for profitable items and then source them. Wholesale involves selling brands that you don't own. So, you'll need to find a registered wholesaler. This also means you don't have to create a listing, which involves taking pictures of the product and writing a title and description. The challenge is, there can be several sellers selling the product under the same listing. Sellers compete for the buy button to make a sale.

Private Label

The private label model is the most expensive to set up. Sellers source a lucrative product from a manufacturer and place their brand on it. You build and own the listing and can report anyone selling under your listing. Sellers take time to find relevant keywords associated with their products. Keywords ensure the product appears when customers type in the search bar. They must be used appropriately throughout the listing.

Why I wrote this book

By the end of this book, my goal is to enable you to make an informed decision. For a person like me, who has an interest in selling on Amazon. After watching a free webinar, was told "...buy this course worth $20k. If you act now get you can have it for $1k. Enjoy access and unlimited support for 12 months! Or your money back." Those free webinars were often not enough for someone to make an informed decision. I decided to write this book so you know what you are getting into.

To get the best out of this book, use it as a learning tool. First, read the entire book and decide if Amazon FBA is for you. Then use the book as a guide by completing the questions. Carry out research through to launching your first private label product.

What makes this book different is you'll have a running total of costs as you read through. So, you can get a rough idea of the level of investment required to launch your first product in your first year.

Included will be links and details of resources I have used on my journey. They are suggestions to give you a starting point. I would encourage you to do your own research before making a decision. Things change every day and by the time of print, I'm sure better options may have sprung up!

Once you have completed the book, refer to the notes you have written here. Use it to keep yourself accountable and motivated.

Crossword Answers

Created using the Crossword Maker on TheTeachersCorner.net

Across

2. Total value of owned items and investments. (**assets**)

5. The return on an investment, often expressed as a percentag (**roi**)

7. Day-to-day expenses incurred to keep a business running. (**operational cost**)

8. Identification number used in the UK for customs purposes (**eori**)

10. Money received from customers. (**receivable**)

Down

1. Profits after all expenses are deducted. (**net profit**)

3. The total profit before deducting expenses. (**gross profit**)

4. The amount of money a business receives in cash. (**cash received**)

6. The flow of money into and out of a business. (**cashflow**)

9. Amount owed to a business. (**debt**)